GREAT PIANO ETUDES

*Masterpieces by Chopin, Scriabin,
Debussy, Rachmaninoff
and Others*

Edited by
DAVID DUTKANICZ

DOVER PUBLICATIONS, INC.
Mineola, New York

Bibliographical Note

This Dover edition, first published in 2006, is a new compilation of works
reproduced from early authoritative editions.

International Standard Book Number: 0-486-45277-8

Manufactured in the United States of America
Dover Publications, Inc., 31 East 2nd Street, Mineola, N.Y. 11501

CONTENTS

Etude No. 3

from Etudes, Op. 10

Frédéric Chopin

Etude No. 6

from Etudes, Op. 10

Frédéric Chopin

Etude No. 9

from Etudes, Op. 10

Frédéric Chopin

Etude No. 12

from Etudes, Op. 10

Frédéric Chopin

Etude No. 1
from Etudes, Op. 25

Frédéric Chopin

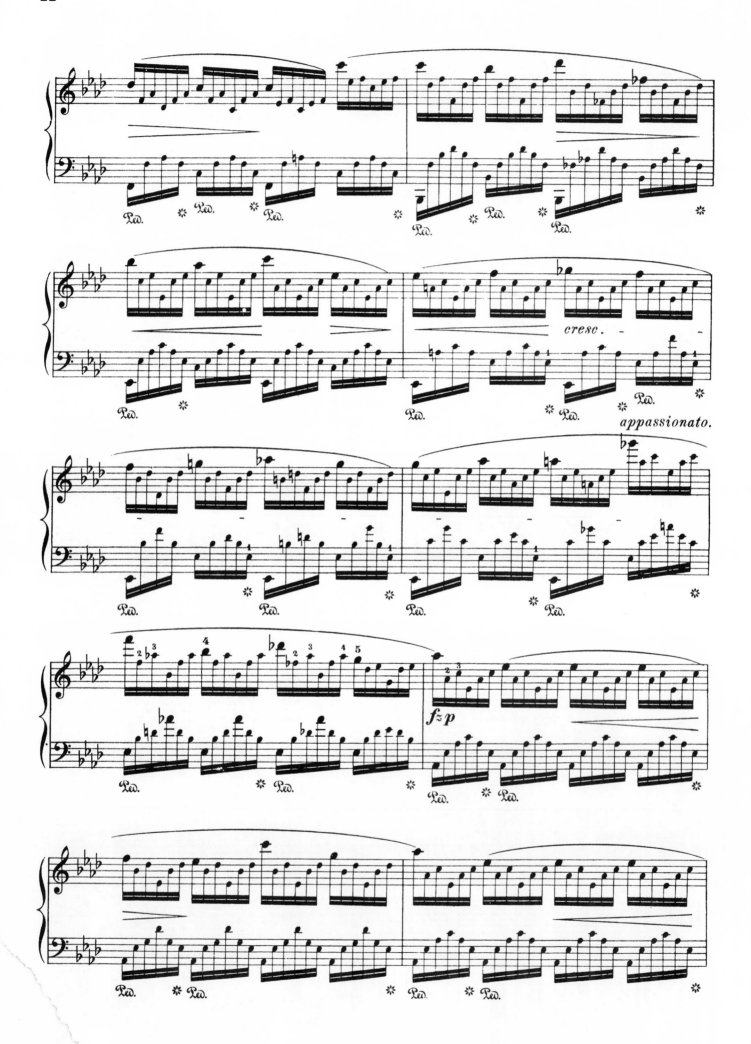

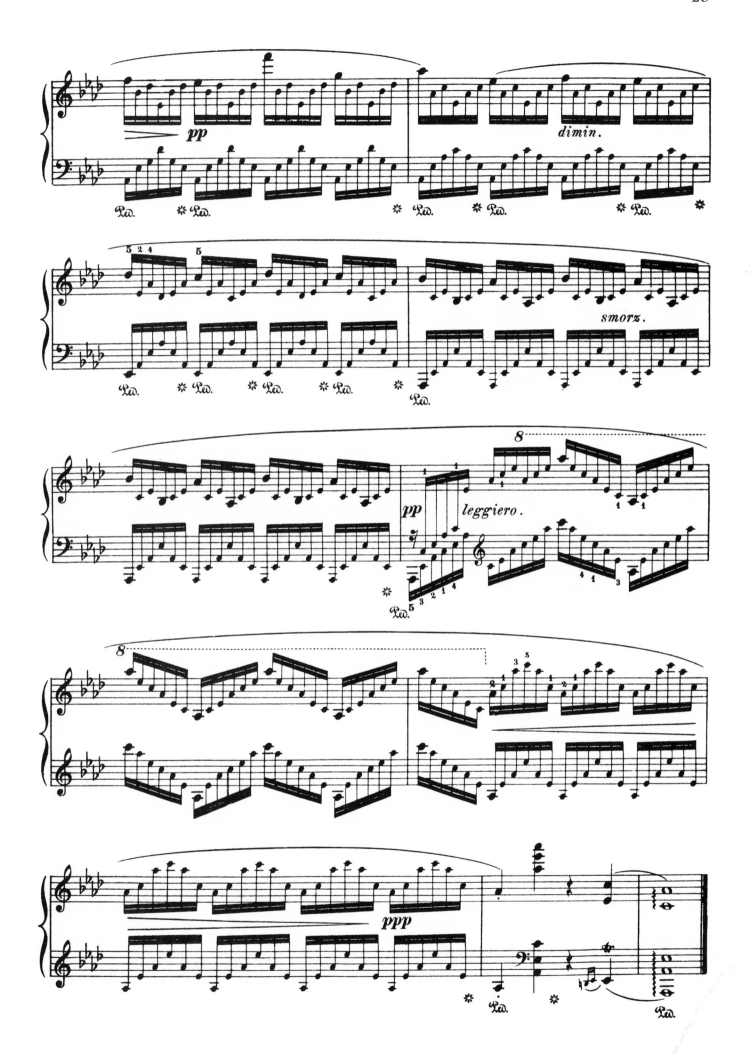

Etude No. 7

from Etudes, Op. 25

Frédéric Chopin

Etude No. 9

from Etudes, Op. 25

Frédéric Chopin

Etude No. 11
from Etudes, Op. 25

Frédéric Chopin

Etude No. 1

from Three New Etudes

Frédéric Chopin

Etude No. 9

from Etude in 12 Exercises, Op. 1

Franz Liszt

Etude No. 12

from Etude in 12 Exercises, Op. 1

Franz Liszt

Etude No. 3, La Campanella

from Etudes for Transcendental Technique after Paganini

Franz Liszt

Etude No. 2

from Paganini Etudes, Op. 10

Robert Schumann

Theme
from Symphonic Etudes, Op. 13

Robert Schumann

Variation No. 1
from Symphonic Etudes, Op. 13

Robert Schumann

Variation No. 4
from Symphonic Etudes, Op. 13

Robert Schumann

Etude No. 1
from Three Etudes, Op. 104b

Felix B. Mendelssohn

Piano Study
after an Etude by Chopin

Johannes Brahms

Etude No. 2
"For Finger Independence"
from Six Etudes, Op. 52

Camille Saint-Saëns

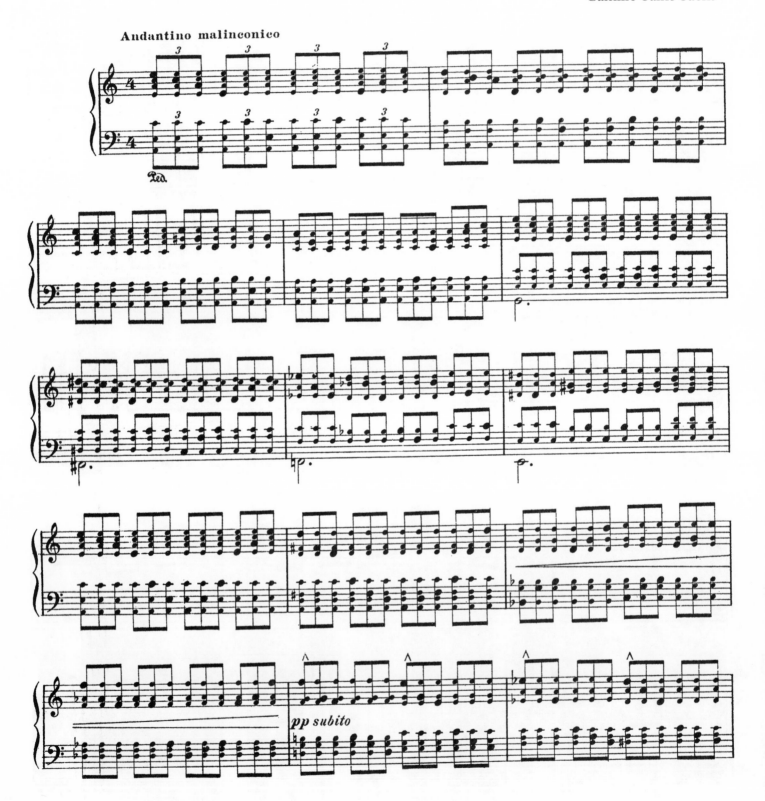

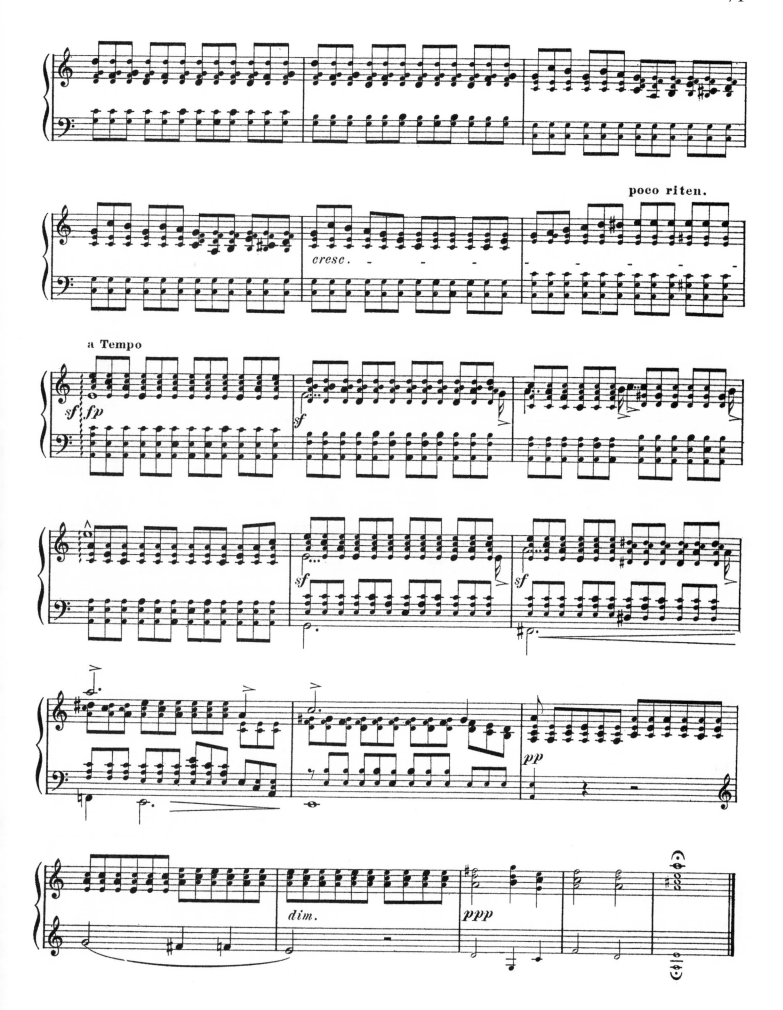

Etude No. 5, Elegy

from Six Etudes for the Left Hand, Op. 135

Camille Saint-Saëns

74

a Tempo
il canto marcato - molto espressivo

(1) *Cet accord ne doit pas être frappé.*
   [This chord must not be struck.]

Etude "Ondine"
Op. 1

Anton Rubinstein

Etude No. 7

from Etudes, Op. 8

Alexander Scriabin

Tempo I

Etude No. 8

from Etudes, Op. 8

Alexander Scriabin

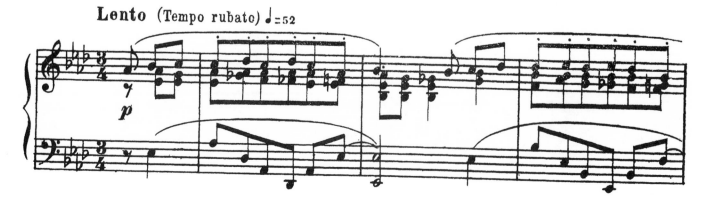

Poco più vivo ♩=66

rubato

sf

sf

1) *pp* (according to the composer's instructions).
2) The dynamic nuances in this passage, according to the
   composer's instructions, are:

pp

Tempo I

3) See note 1.♩

4) *cresc.*
5) *p* } according to the composer's instructions.

6) See note 1.

7) - - -
8) **pp** } according to the composer's instructions.
9) *calando*

Etude No. 4
from Etudes, Op. 42

Alexander Scriabin

Etude No. 7
from Etudes, Op. 42

Alexander Scriabin

Etude No. 1

from Twelve Etudes

Claude Debussy

Etude No. 3

from Twelve Etudes

Claude Debussy

Etude No. 10
from Twelve Etudes

Claude Debussy

Etude No. 3

from Four Etudes, Op. 4

Karol Szymanowski

Tempo I.

Etude No. 2
from Etudes-Tableaux, Op. 33

Serge Rachmaninoff

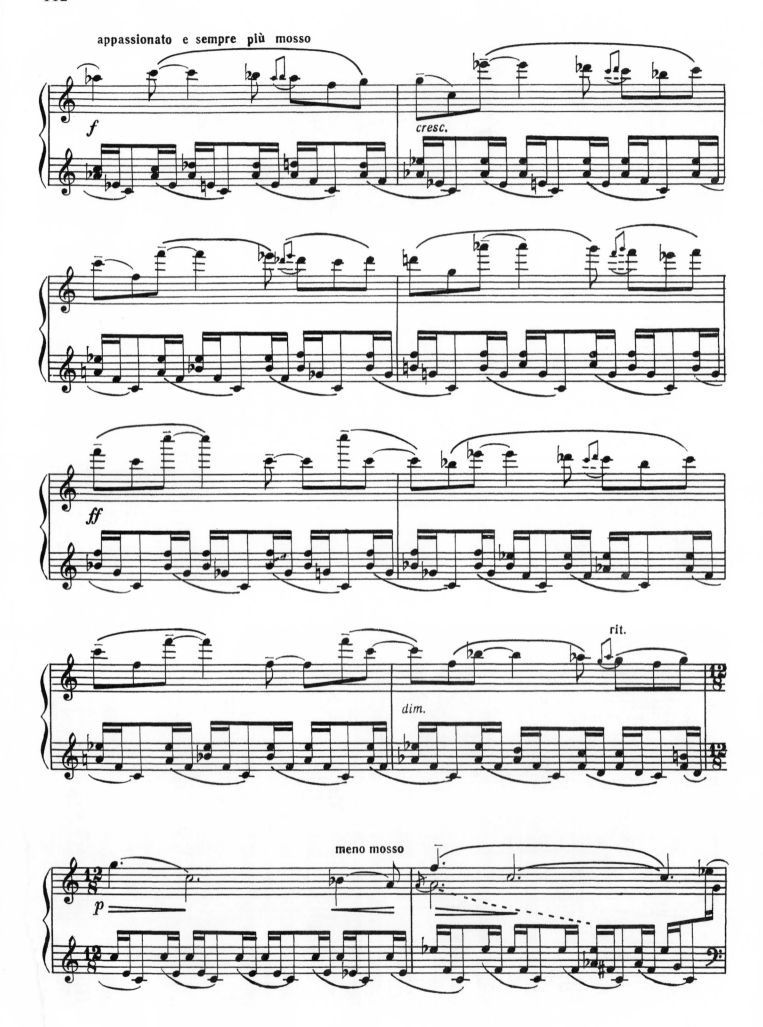

Etude No. 4

from Etudes-Tableaux, Op. 33

Serge Rachmaninoff

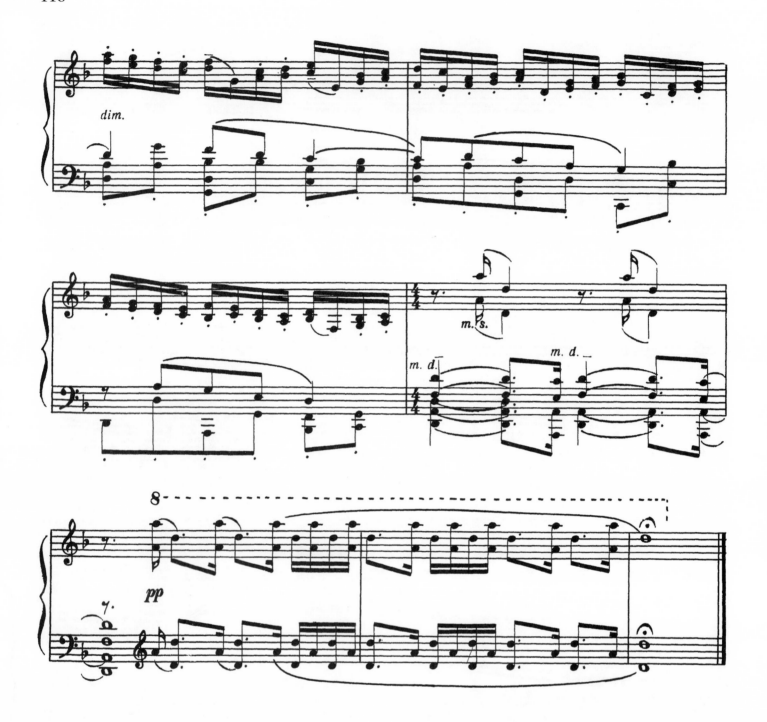

Etude No. 2
from Etudes-Tableaux, Op. 33

Serge Rachmaninoff